Poetry From Northern England

Edited by Angela Fairbrace

First published in Great Britain in 2007 by:
Forward Press Ltd.
Remus House
Coltsfoot Drive
Peterborough
PE2 9JX
Telephone: 01733 898108
Website: www.forwardpress.co.uk

All Rights Reserved

Copyright Contributors 2006

SB ISBN 1 84418 453 6

Foreword

Forward Press was established in 1989 to provide a platform for poets to showcase their works. Today, Forward Press continues to provide an outlet for new and established poets and *Poetry From Northern England* is tribute to this.

Poetry should be interesting and, above all else, accessible to all. Forward Press publications are for all lovers of traditional verse and of the art of rhyme, as well as for those who enjoy contemporary verse. *Poetry From Northern England* showcases both styles ensuring a varied read, and proving traditional and modern do complement each other.

Poetry From Northern England proudly showcases the region's best poets and the joy and inspiration we can all draw from where we live.

Contents

Dreamstealer	J Wilson	1
Behind Vacant Eyes	Clare Todd	2
The Circus	Dorothy Yates	3
The Laird And His Lady	Margaret Sanderson	4
Supernatural Dawn	Owen Reed	5
Banks Of The Tyne	Kathleen Potter	6
The End	Liane McGovern	7
The Medallion	Ann Pickering	8
The Capital Of Culture	June Cameron	9
You Never Knew	Sandra Robson	10
Familiar Place	Helen Smith	11
Land Of My Heart	E D Bowen	12
Thoughts From A Bridge Over River	Kathleen Guess	13
Brit 'Ish'	Saqib Hussain	14
Voyage	David Bury	15
Movie Magic	Tracy Somers	16
Darker Times	Barbara Sanderson	18
The Lakes	Peter Corbett	19
Life's An Adventure	Teresa Smith	20
The Lakeland Hills	Margery Rayson	21
Reminiscing	Mary B Tyrer	22
Pride Of Place	Shirley Temple Beckett	23
Long, Lazy Summers	Ann Hogg	24
Flight Of Beauty	David Bridgewater	25
Listening	Yvonne Carsley	26
A Gift	Starchild	27
The Sea	Tess McHugh	28
Blue Oasis	Steven Morris	29
The Haven That's Ours	Sandra Griesbach	30
Too Close For Comfort	Elaine Edgar	31
My Garden	Barbara Vera Sleath	32
Dreams Are Real	J P Armour	33
Sunflower	Anita McErlean	34
Second Chance	Dorothy Rowe	35
The Colour Of The Seasons	Debbie Goodman	36
Age	Gwyneth Jones	37
Another Place	Angela M Schroder	38
Joy Of Cumbria	B W Ballard	39
The Battle For My Mind	A P Richardson	40

Title	Author	Page
My Wonderful Dad	Kenneth Pendlebury	41
Next February	T I Hill	42
A Poem For Mum	Joan Beer	43
Wonderings	Vivienne Joyce	44
Cumberland Song	Mary Dimond	45
The Simple Life	Jackie Richardson	46
St Barnabas' Diamond Jubilee - A Thanksgiving	Rita Robinson	47
The Dragonfly	Martin Jenkins	48
Aunt Maude Blues	Pauline Ilsley	49
Skyline	William Reilly	50
A Dog's Best Friend	Beryl Thornbury	51
Travel'er	Gail Rowan	52
Brindleheath	Philip Loudon	53
Tears Of Life	Jennie Stott	54
Home Is Where The Heart Is	David Hamey	55
I See You!	Andrew Rawlings	56
The Fall	Denise Southern	57
April 23rd	Brian Lees	58
Write It Down, So It's Not Forgotten	Jean K Washbourne	59
A Light Shines On Blackburn In Lancashire	Crystal Waters	60
Blackpool Tower	Hope Bunton	61
Lonesome	Peggy Johnson	62
Through The Haze	Burgess Jay Barrow	63
Reina Of The Marshes	Christine Dodding	64
Ethereal Pause	Di Wade	65
A Day Beside The Sea	Olwen Hornby	66
A Special Time	S J Davidson	67
Lancashire, My Lancashire	Adrian Yates	68
George's Ghost	Eric Holt	69
Museum Of Hope	Peter Rigg	70
Grandson Without A Dad	Nancy Reeves	72
Resolution	Joan Evans	73
Manchester Melancholy	Alison E Holland	74
We Have Been Everywhere	Winifred Smith	76
Closing Doors	Lynn Brookes	77
A Lancashire Lass	Ivy Jackson	78
Whit Monday In Runcorn	Violet Astbury	80
Memory Lane	Mavis Wright	82
Pauline	T McFarlane	84

Title	Author	Page
Home	Graeme Doherty	85
Safe Within	Nona Watt	86
Blessed Silver Chimes	Thomas Hull	87
Baby	Kelly Darbyshire	88
The Poppy	June Hardman	90
Thoughts	Florence C Watkinson	91
Bygone Days	Rita Smith	92
Accents	Mavis Catlow	94
Honk If You Love The Lord	G Snowdon	95
The Whispering Trade ...	Emily Blyth	96
How Bizarre	Malcolm Lisle	97
Northumberland Street	Kenneth Mood	98
Litterbugs	Jean Cumbor	99
Full Circle	Clare Thompson-Lewis	100
The Run	R F Trollope	101
Bamburgh Castle	H J Slaiter	102
A Midsummer Moment	P J Wilson	103
The Rosy Cross	Peter Bramwell	104
The Dream	Richard Alan Long	105
Bryony Reads The Newspaper To Grandad	Bob Goodall	106
Exmoor - My Garden Of Eden	Patrick J Horrell	107
Feelings	M M Armstrong	108
Crossroads	Beth Spinks	109
An Ode To Jarrovians Everywhere	Duncan Robson	110
Remember Terri Schiavo	Robert Henry Lonsdale	111
Final Lullaby	Scott Maclean	112
Just Passing Through	Kate Bylett	113
Today's Bairns	John Stenhouse	114
The Jigsaw Of Life	W H Spry	116
Dualism	Robin Bailey	117
A Life Of No Account	Pauline Fazackerley	118
Ladybirds	Nicola Daly	119
The Tea Dance	Joan Wheeler	120
I Remember	Greta Forsyth	121
A Teardrop From Heaven	Elizabeth A Wilkinson	122
Beast	Glenda Stryker	123

The Poems

Dreamstealer

Don't steal my dreams
They're not in mode,
You need a bold
Less nebulous style,
Custom-made with
Space between the
Pleats of the cyber
Kind, the net a wider
Mesh than mine, stop,
Don't come so close!
Illegal act, you may annex,
You alarm, my dreams
Don't want to change
Their line to meet your needs,
They like the comfort of
The known, a band of broad
Design to keep your area
Well defined could solve
The current issue in dispute.
So just go away
And leave them be and
Leave my dreams to me.

J Wilson

Behind Vacant Eyes

Here in my mind
There's a spider making webs,
A moth flitting by,
As I lazily watch
From behind vacant eyes.
It's said I have an empty mind,
But if they could see,
In these dank caverns
The brightness of twisted memories,
That lay scattered in the darkness.
Behind vacant eyes.
Thoughts racing through,
Visions shattered,
Attracting the moth,
Caught by the spider,
Sucking the life.
Behind vacant eyes.

Clare Todd (Warrington)

The Circus

When t' circus come to Heywood
Ee, I knew I'd have to go.
Fer I love to see them animals
That they allus have in t' show.
Now it said in t' Advertiser
That seats were 50p,
But if you were a pensioner
Then a lot of 'em were free.
So I took misself to t' Bit Bats
Cos that's wer t' show were on.
I found mi seat and sat mi down
And waited for the fun.
There were mums and dads and lots o' kids
All laughing loud and long.
There were elephants and crazy clowns
An' a seal that sang a song.
There were horses too wi' swishing tails
And lions roaring wild.
There were beautiful girls upon a trapeze
And a chimp dressed like a child.
Ee a did enjoy misself
But then a knew a would
For a love all that excitement
And have often wished a could
Be part of all that circus scene
And march around the town
But a've just remembered
A'm much too old (85)
To act like a circus clown.

Dorothy Yates (Heywood)

The Laird And His Lady

This story that I'm about to unfold
Is almost two hundred and fifty years old
Please listen with feeling and try not to jest
For the soul of this man is unable to rest

This man was a 'Laird' of a country estate
But its value meant nothing, when he knew of his fate
He'd wed, just that day, a wife he adored
Their future beginning, his happiness soared

Then, after the service, the couple and guests
Played hide-and-seek, while others laid bets
There were so many nooks, in that vast castle ground
That the Laird's fine Lady, just couldn't be found

He carried on looking, when the others had left
He searched high and low, frantic, bereft
The hours passed by and then there were days
His spirit was torn, in all different ways

He kept the drapes closed, to shut out the light
And cried himself softly to sleep every night
With the passage of time, he came to assume
His wife had deserted him, that afternoon

So great was his sorrow, that soon he passed on
But his sobs had been heard, long after he'd gone
And some years later, the castle was sold
But the buyers could never get rid of the cold

And up in the attic, they found a huge chest
Containing a skeletal figure, at rest
The clasp had dropped down, on the Lady inside
Entombing within, that Laird's lovely bride

A brand new Inn will be opening soon
Built from that ancient castle ruin
And the cries of the Laird and his Lady's soft weeping
Will be heard by its guests, while they're meant to be sleeping . . .

Margaret Sanderson (South Shields)

Supernatural Dawn

Caressing cloud that hugs the hidden heights,
A craving lover jealous of the dawn,
That falls and soaks in sheets of shining light,
To break the hold of might and mist at morn.

A flash of brilliance hits the lower land,
As if a god is angered by the bright;
His angry gleam of diamond eyes demand,
The leaving of encroaching day for night!

The hills surrender to the clouds' delight,
Exquisite rape, the drenching grey that grows,
Seducing strength from the hills that throws,
The sullen sun back into sunken night.

But once the god has loved and caring kissed,
He leaves the hills to rest for love again,
Then rolling down the sides in mystic mists,
An eerie avalanche of greying rain.

Owen Reed

Banks Of The Tyne

Angel of the North still in her prime
Outstretched arms embracing a northern clime
Inscrutable, she dominates skyline
Greeting visitors to banks of the Tyne.
Awestruck small children demand to know why
The rusty lady has no wings to fly.

Gateshead triumphant has come of age
Playing cultural host to the saucy Sage
A young jezebel with curious grace
Music divine spanning age, time and taste.
The Baltic, prim and proper maiden aunt
Status threatened by cheeky debutante.

Designer with sense of mischievous
Gifted a heritage ingenious –
Tilting bridge with sultry blinking eye
Wickedly winking as small craft slip by
Its walkway spanning two Cities of Pride
Like the wedding bands of a groom and bride.

Newcastle's cityscape melds new and old
Antique elegance versus trendy bold.
Alfresco diners bask in fading light
Caressed by indigo shadows of night.
Lovers embraced by a feather-soft breeze
Caught for eternity on artist's frieze.

Sun bleeds on morsels of chips and ice cream
A beggar's banquet befitting a queen
Raucous warring gulls slicing the quiet
Like brazen harlots inciting a riot.
Becalmed and serene, mirroring the scene
A once dirty Tyne now sparkles pristine.

Kathleen Potter (South Shields)

The End

The closer the end comes,
The harder it is to do it.
My heart is screaming,
It can't take this pain anymore.
The darkness is closing in,
But I can't wait any longer.
The time has come to end it all,
The poison will run through my veins.
My red tears will flow,
The tight rope will burn my skin.
The wind will rush as I fall,
I'll gasp as my last breath escapes.

Liane McGovern (Yarm)

The Medallion

Standing on the quayside,
At early morning light,
In driving rain and vicious wind,
The ship sailed out of sight,
With her beloved son.

She prayed for him in churches,
For God to be his guide
And asked the saints' protections,
As he journeyed far and wide,
To bring him safely home.

The silver medal round his neck,
Her parting gift of love,
St Christopher, the patron saint,
Protect him from above,
Wherever he may sail.

For many years he sailed the seas
And swiftly through the ranks he rose,
Surviving bullets, fire and flood,
He lived and loved the life he chose,
Many times around the world.

Time took its toll, so he retired
And settled on the coast,
But gazing out to sea, recalled,
The life he loved the most,
With no regrets.

The medal now is smooth and thin,
But worn with greatest pride,
In memory of the mariner,
Who sailed on the early tide,
Into another world.

Ann Pickering (Sunderland)

The Capital Of Culture

The Capital of Culture, we didn't win,
But we think the north-east, is a great place to live in.
It may have escaped the judge's eye,
To our Angel of the North, over sixty foot high.
The artist creator, was Antony Gormley,
With its arms outstretched, greeting visitors warmly.

The Millennium Bridge, called the blinking eye,
Opens up, to let ships pass by,
Its rainbow of colours, when lit up at night,
Its reflection on the water, makes a wonderful sight.
The Tyne Bridge is our landmark, for which we are well known,
A comforting sight to know you are home.

They may think our City is a non-starter,
But we've moved on, since the film, 'Get Carter',
We've got History, Cathedrals, beautiful Countryside,
Lots of transformations on the quayside.
Bars, Restaurants, the Baltic, music centre on song,
On both sides of the Tyne, lots going on.

Cloth caps, brown ale, is the image, seen to portray,
But that went out with Florrie, who took Andy Capp away.
Our weather may be cold, but the Geordie welcome warm,
We are friendly people, with our Geordie dialect.
When visitors come to our City,
Their holiday memories are, just *perfect!*

June Cameron (Gateshead)

You Never Knew

(Dedicated to my brother-in-law, Robert, who sadly passed away 17th August, 2006)

You never knew
That life lived for just a moment
Then in a blink was gone,
Yet the soul lives forever
It's with us, where it belongs.
Love is for eternity
It will never go away,
Warming and surrounding us
Always sure to stay.
Our memories are what we cherish
We store them like a book,
Take them out when we feel sad
Enjoy another look.
You never knew
That he would leave you
Causing so much pain,
Making all the tears flow
Just like falling rain.
Yet the friendship that you cherished
Is yours alone to keep,
Never leaving you alone
Not even while you sleep.
Feel his breath, his tender touch
That comes from up above,
You will never be without him
He will cover you in love.
Never-ending, never gone
Always strong and true,
Robert will be forever
Standing there with you.

Sandra Robson (Newcastle)

Familiar Place

The winding wheel stands tall and proud,
As the cage devours the waiting crowd.
The blackened faces newly risen,
Handing back the tokens given.

Overhead, on wires in view,
Pass bucketfuls of coal they've hewn.
There, behind the buildings lag,
The smouldering mounds of shale and slag.

The assembly hut as quiet as a grave,
No hooter today, no men to save.
Women wrapped in shawls of grey,
Waiting to collect their husband's pay.

Looking down on chimney pots,
With night lights shining on little cots,
The men tread wearily, village bound,
To bathe, eat and walk the greyhound.

Grubby children play in rhyme,
Dancing games amid the grime.
They stop to watch the men go home,
Secretly thankful when they see their own.

Helen Smith (Darlington)

Land Of My Heart

The Irish tell of their hillsides green
The Welsh of their mountains tall
The Scots of their woods and lochs serene
But I love England best of all.

For I've travelled all over Scotland
And into the depths of Wales
I've seen many films on Ireland
But my heart, it lies in the Dales.

Where the lanes are lined with dry-stone walls
And the verges are covered in flowers
And friendly folk pass the time of day
That's where I like to spend my hours.

I love to be where the river Tees flows
Or where moors roll up to the sky
In pastures where the Blue gentian grows
And the Lapwing and Curlew cry.

E D Bowen (Darlington)

Thoughts From A Bridge Over River

River water is like laughter
Rippling gently on the air.
Swirling, curling, moving faster
Music that we all can share.
Flowing calmly on the level
Where fish swim within the pool
Its voice is like a minor treble
Sounding light and sweet and cool
Till it nears its journey's ending
Coursing onwards to the sea
Symphony of rushing water
Turned to loud and major key.
Storms can raise their voice to anger
Waves as high as mighty towers
Heaving, battering, bringing danger
Under leaden skies that glower
But today in summer daylight
Trickling, gurgling, pleasant stream
Wavelets dancing in the sunlight
On the bridge I sit and dream.
Lightly bubbling, running water
In and out the rocks it darts
Ageless, constant, like God's laughter
Finding echoes in my heart.

Kathleen Guess (Stockton-on-Tees)

Brit 'Ish'

I would like to write about where I'm from
Although I'm sometimes confused where that is
You see, I'm from the North of England – Manchester
But also of Asian heritage

When I tell people I'm from Manchester
Seeing me as Asian, they may ask where I'm 'originally' from
Seeing me as British, people in Asia may think the same
So I'm sometimes confused as to where I belong

Is there a place called 'Britasia'?
Can't find it on the map
Can you see?
I've heard it's full of Brit 'ish' people
And curry on chips is the national delicacy

What defines Britishness?
Birthplace? Skin colour? Name?
Or is it something sports related –
Like the passion with which you watch a football game?

Or to be comfortable with your own and other people's
Culture, roots and identity?
Maybe that's part of being a complete citizen?
Maybe that's what being British means?

In fact, that's what Britain is
A mix of cultures, lots of diversity
And having written my feelings, I'd like to relax, unwind
With a nice cup of tea!

Saqib Hussain (Manchester)

Voyage

Aboard the ship, Ocean Breeze,
Riding on the crest of a wave.
Cutting through the deep blue seas,
On a voyage to the lady I constantly crave.

When darkness started to fall
And the stars began to appear.
Heading ever closer to a squall,
In the face of which I will show
No fear.

For on the other side of that storm,
Is the lady I love very much.
To feel, once again, through my uniform,
Her tender, loving touch.

David Bury (Manchester)

Movie Magic

Looking back through the years
all those fine actors and actresses.
Musicals and melodramas,
tap shoes and backing crews.
Shining lights and a
million magic moments.

Leading ladies,
lighting up the screen.
Hayworth, Monroe, Hepburn, Kelly,
screen goddesses,
Always looking a
million dollars.

Curtain calls
dressing rooms filled with
Edith Head costumes.
Visions of beauty in
satin and velvet;
gliding across that silver screen.
Lights! Camera! Action!

Hollywood heroes,
dashing and handsome.
Gable, Cagney, Stewart, Wayne.
Rugged of jaw and
stiff upper lip.
Always there to save the day
riding up in a
Blaze of Glory!

Where did it all go
the glitz and glamour of
yesteryear?
When did we stop believing
in all the
razzamatazz?
Now it's all just a memory;
that Golden Age of Hollywood!

Aged reruns flow across our
plasma screens.
All the oldies but goodies,
still alive in our hearts;
but slowly sinking,
eclipsed by a new age.
Hi-tech movie epics;
million dollar, computer generated
special effects.
But like the old song says,
'That's Entertainment'!

Tracy Somers (Warrington)

Darker Times

Distant lonely voices
They echo through my head
Replaying conversations
Words already said
A soundtrack of regret
These twisted melodies
Sandman, deliver me from
Darker times like these

The bedroom clock says 3am
But sleep is nowhere near
As clouds drift across the moon
Dark shadows shift in here
Cigarette smoke and mirrors
The ghosts of memories
Oh, spirit me away from
Darker times like these

Dawn hides round the corner
Of this night's darkest hour
The time is late, I'm still awake
As the clock strikes four
And the wind talks in whispers
As it creeps between the trees
It's speaking of secrets
And darker times like these.

Barbara Sanderson (Aspatria)

The Lakes

The billow-white sails
Proudly running
Into the Windermere wind:
Frozen in time
With painted oils
Hanging, eternal,
On flock-covered walls.

The Langdale's snow-dusted peaks
Star-pointing to higher realms;
With forests to bear the soul in
And hanging rocks near,
Living there on the edge
Of Enlightenment,
Whiling away the days
Each a universe in miniature,
As the swaying daffodils
Herald a rebirth
Of a God-sent idyll.

We hanker after peace
In the ever-spinning wheel;
And yet here for free
The meaning of bliss
Is everywhere experienced.
For, with the Eagle's eye
The land below is seen
Verdant without pretence
Cycling in a seasonal round:
For we are more in touch
With our real selves
When we feel its presence
As we walk its hallowed ground.

Peter Corbett (Liverpool)

Life's An Adventure

My brother and I, when we were small
Enjoyed throwing stones over the wall.
Our neighbour's back wall was ever so high
Us being small, it reached up to the sky.
Our little game was to get that stone
Over the wall and into the unknown.
We didn't know of another family
A few doors away, by the name of Bramley.
That is where our stones come to lay
In the area where the children would play.
We were playing one day, when we heard the call
A very loud voice came over that wall.
'What are you children playing at?
You've just scared the life out of the cat!'
There was no more throwing stones for us
We didn't know there'd be such a fuss.
'Didn't you realise the danger?' Mam said
'You could've hit someone on the head!'
So our game had to stop, but we soon found another
It didn't take long for me and my brother.
We became Batman and Robin, climbing that wall
Until another mishap – I had a fall.
That didn't stop us looking for adventure
We almost gave me mam early dementia!
But childhood doesn't last long enough
Soon you're an adult and the going gets tough
Children's pastimes today, their memories will be
Of playing computer games or watching TV.
They should be looking for adventure and having a ball
As long as they're not throwing stones over a wall!

Teresa Smith (Liverpool)

The Lakeland Hills

Wind-kissed autumn rain
refreshed my inner sanctuary
walking through the Lakeland Hills
in gratifying solitude
I pondered on a place of peace
with no redeeming thoughts of you
my heart it soared up to the skies
with words expressed to sanctify
A grateful happy country life
myself alone in paradise
I praise the hills and lakes
to complete my life's ambitions.

Margery Rayson (Ulverston)

Reminiscing

The garden is my oasis
The route that is my calm
Majestic oaks, colourful shrubs
Cat's on roof, away from harm
As twilight comes, I reminisce
Of times so long ago
Beauteous thoughts consume my mind
As they continue to flow
Passion for arts, ballet was mine
I love the then and now
I watch the glorious sunset
My family's my real love now.

Mary B Tyrer (Liverpool)

Pride Of Place

Cheshire is not only famous for her cheese
And shopkeepers who aim to please
The beauty of her countryside
Will make your eyes open wide
From hillside to grassy dales
Historians still tell their tales
The heart of this special place
Is how the folks to you relate
Warm hearts and friendly faces
Are hard to find in other places
There's more to Cheshire than meets the eye
The young have brains, we can't deny
Intelligence inherited from industrial pioneers
Who put Cheshire on the map
And thrived for their ideas?
You know it was a country place
Until they discovered soap
With haste, it grew into a thriving land
Near the Mersey's golden sands
Polish, Irish, English, worked side by side
Industry was born, how it thrived
With sweat and tears they toiled each day for
Each generation they paved the way
Times right now are far from good
Although we've done all we could
So much we have attained and more
Piece by piece we can restore
Pride of place and place of pride
With inner strength we'll turn the tide.

Shirley Temple Beckett (Widnes)

Long, Lazy Summers

Long, lazy summers,
Clear blue skies,
Playing two balls up the wall
Up the road in Mayfield Rise.

Climbing into playgrounds,
Deserted, silence reigns.
Scrambling onto ledges,
Peering through grubby panes.

Holidays at Dover Court
Mum, Dad and me.
Sleeping in a caravan
Where we could see the sea.

Twisted metal, fire and flames
Torched the camp at night.
Molten coins from arcade games
Scavengers delight.

Creeping into churches,
Incense and Holy Water.
Chalices and crosses
Decorate the altar.

From the gloom a priest appears
To chase us kids away
He baptises her, Elaine that is,
That night, to God I pray.

Tosh liked eating brushes
Unwinding toilet rolls
Eating chairs and teddy bears
And playing with my dolls.

These are my memories
As fresh as the day.
Little Tosh is fast asleep
Mum and Dad, passed away.

Ann Hogg (Southport)

Flight Of Beauty

I saw a dream
Embrace my eye
A dream that was a butterfly
Whose wings did beat
Like a lullaby
Whose flight of beauty lit the sky

Just like a prayer
My thoughts invoke
It took to flight when dawn awoke
Into my garden
Where birds elope
I saw this sublime soul approach

Above the flowers
And through the trees
Its very presence hushed the breeze
Dressed in colours
Whose glimpse I seize
That settled on the eye to please

A precious creature
In emerald-green
Fluttering in and out my dream
Whose erratic journey
Kissed the scene
Before settling near my self-esteem

At my feet
It came to rest
And stayed awhile at my request
With refreshed wings
Time to impress
It resumed upon its leisurely quest

And now the dream
That blessed my lawn
Now leaves the scene, nature had drawn
Whose wings did sing
Like a ballad born
Whose flight of beauty touched the dawn.

David Bridgewater (Wallasey)

Listening

Floating here above the Earth
I listen to the voices below

Cries of anguish
Cries of joy
Pleas for help
And exclamations of delight

I hear the sobbing
I hear the laughter
Expressions of pain
And sighs of pleasure

So much noise
So much chaos

Dreams and wishes
Hopes and fears
Shouts and screams
Life and death

I hear it all
And I hear you.

Yvonne Carsley (Manchester)

A Gift

As you watch and listen, transfixed by the awesome
Scene in front of you. An array of deep vibrant
Colours encompasses you and fills your soul with
The everlasting rays of creation. You can hear your
Heart sing in pure delight.

The peace and tranquillity carry you away deeper
Into oblivion, uplifting you to a state of pure ecstasy.
Ready to be enchanted by the magic and wonder in
This truly glorious dimension. A gift of pure divinity
For all those who wish to experience it.

Let the atmosphere envelop your soul. Feel the
Freedom as you enter into the vastness of this
Resplendent dimension full of eternal treasures
To satisfy the mind, body and soul. Bringing
Them together in perfect harmony.

Starchild (Warrington)

The Sea

The sea reminds me of days we walked together
The beautiful memories we shared,
In troubled times we fought and cried together
Your life has gone but mine was spared,
Years were long, yet fast when we compared.
Captured moments make me sigh
Forgotten kisses make me cry,
Tears flood my face, I want to die.
I can't help wondering why
The way you had to die.
As I watch the tide go out
At the ending of the day,
My heart leaps and yearns,
But you have passed away.

Tess McHugh (Liverpool)

Blue Oasis

There exists for a few days only,
In a secret wood, some think lonely.
One of those hidden magic places,
A perfectly perfumed, private oasis.

Not far from the city and the noise,
Where hard-working busy girls and boys.
Know nothing of what lies nearby,
Each year miss their chance to spy . . .

An ephemeral carpet of richest blue,
Bluebell springtime and in with the new.
A display on show for a day or two,
Which is just for me and just for you.

Steven Morris (Sandbach)

The Haven That's Ours

Old leafy lanes, there are now but a few
Some local wildlife, but they have our measure
Beautiful gardens, floral parks and green land
Makes living here much more than a pleasure.

Grand trees that surround our quaint avenues
Look like stairs up to Heaven from here on the Earth
Most provide homes for grey squirrel and bird
Portraying great strength and aware of their worth.

The dwellings around our unique neighbourhood
Reflect, like a mirror, the lifestyle from within
Some alone, or in clusters, others joined at the hip
Some hidden beneath an ancient green skin.

Our village can boast a wide mixture of souls
Who constantly ride on life's merry-go-round
From those long retired and now living alone
To the young, whose music, most would impound.

Families with children greet friends at the gate
Pets join the fun as they hear laughter in play
And our environment loses that special surprise
As familiarity replaces the initial bouquet.

Seen as perfection in bright summer sun
Less so, as skies darken for showers
Everyone knows, from brand new to the old
This place: it's the haven that's ours.

Sandra Griesbach (Manchester)

Too Close For Comfort

Old bones observe the walking aid propped up by the door
I reach for the remote and wish I could 'run' once more . . .
How do we survive what we 'see'?
The horrors and the carnage
Daily observers spoon-feed the horrors on TV
But incapable of being heard against bombardment and unrest.
My life too has left me reeling at times, as loved ones passed.
The weight of the world seemed to drift in and out like fog
My 'true grit' got called into account many times
As life dealt blow after blow, but what do I really 'know' -
Of the suffering of war-torn regions, back street hovels or
endless desert plains where every drop of water is sacred -
carried for days on fragile limbs.
Questions leave my lips unheard in the din from the screen
The gunfire, heat and dust a daily diet mixed with hate, it seems.
I silently weep at the atrocities incapable of clearly defining them.
My thoughts shattered by the scenes, they never seem to stop.
These are human beings barely existing, but many are not.
Daily they live with a backdrop of chaos, famine and
inhuman *suffering*
And here am I . . . powerless to do more than answer appeals
in an envelope
Wondering if it will ever make a difference in the scheme of things?
Time felt precious once, when fields surrounded me like a
comforting cloak.
Scraps of those memories remain, vestiges of yesterday when
I breathed the 'essences' of life on the summer breeze and filled my
soul with wild humanity.
Whatever happened to those carefree times?
Why did the purpose cloud and destruction reign?
Why did we *let* it?

Elaine Edgar (Workington)

My Garden

How I love my garden
Especially at night
When all is turned to silver
By the pale moon's light.

I love it in the morning
The sparkling on the dew
As the sun is dawning
On a day that's new.

I love it in the evening
When it goes dark and quiet
Then I hear the night train rushing by,
The Dog Fox calling for a mate
The Vixen's answering cry.

I love it at all times of year
As the seasons come and go
Spring, Summer, Autumn
And in Winter's fall of snow.
How lucky I am to have a garden
That I may love it so.

Barbara Vera Sleath (Wilmslow)

Dreams Are Real

Last night I dreamt of walking
On a strange and lonely shore
Remembering things and people
I thought would come no more

Though no one walked there with me
I still was not alone
For all those friends seemed to be there
The ones I'd long since known

And in my dreams we talked of things
That happened long ago
Joys and sorrows, laughs and tears
Places we used to go

Sights we saw in golden days
Still fresh within our minds
That song, that dance, that sunset
These are the ties that bind

For love of life is precious
And when it's time to go
Those treasured times will be with us
With those friends of long ago

Being old has compensations
Memories grow clear
And when I woke I found I had
A store of happy years

I quite look forward to the time
When I can meet them all
Again we'll be together
In the fairest place of all.

J P Armour (Barrow-in-Furness)

Sunflower

Do you have such contempt for me
To leave me withering like a weed
In the midst of a great sunflower?
Is your contempt such that I am
Nothing but a mild presence
Like a gentle breeze on a bed of corn?
You simply turn on me your back
Your eyes averted, their gaze a-cast!
The sunflower, her beauty akin to perfection
She blinds your averted eyes!
Do you not see me?
Is your heart blind?
See me! Behind you is your path
Look back and see your way
For I, though not a sunflower
Am the greatest flower of all
I am the rose!

Anita McErlean (Manchester)

Second Chance

I had my lungs done in 2005 and
Thank God, I'm here, I am alive.
I live my life day by day,
For with my family I want to stay.
The Doctors and Nurses who brought me through,
Are a wonderful, fantastic team, a brilliant crew.
God bless you all!
And for the lady who gave me a second chance,
My life back,
Thank you with all my heart, dear friend,
For all that you have done
And your family's courage in that hard time,
The gift of life, a precious thing.
I hold myself tall and often sing.
To breathe the fresh air and the scent of the flowers,
The grass, the sweetness of bouquets, I shed a tear,
As I think of all the help and care
And I close my eyes in silent prayer.
Thank you for my life.

Dorothy Rowe (Widnes)

The Colour Of The Seasons

Yellow
It surprises me one day as it grows through the green
It comes in the form of daffodils and to me,
They are the symbol of spring
But as quickly as it comes, the yellow disappears
However, hope is gained with new life
And sounds made by the birds that one will hear.
Red
It burns the earth beneath my feet
But on its way, a relief from his intense heat
It drenches me, yet I need more of this rain on my face
And after, fresh calm is the scent that fills the rest of the day
As the night draws in, I look up at the sky
A sense of anticipation grows, as I wonder
What colour will the sunset be tonight?
Brown
It first emerges with shades of yellow, orange and red
But as life declines, it will fall onto its brown bed
And there, almost untouched, those who feel will remain
Until they are swept away by the unwelcome wind and rain
But this is not the only message that brown does know
As brown makes way for new green to one day show.
White
Like a veil of soft cotton, it covers everything in sight
A deceptive beauty that will cut through you like a knife
One could blemish this beauty by a mere step into the night
The only warmth that seeps into my bitter monochrome space,
Is a smile that will spread swiftly across my face
As I witness the crystal-like stars that pierce into the
never-ending dark
I think to myself, 'I like my little place.'

Debbie Goodman (Middlewich)

Age

Eyes are dim, joints are sore,
Safety chain secures the door,
Locked in me a girl of twenty,
For whom life holds a promise of plenty.
Where have they gone, the flying years?
Passed on a whirl of laughter and tears.
Thirty, forty winging past,
How the years have flown so fast,
But sometimes still I look and see
The pretty girl who once was me.
Age can be cruel yet also kind,
I'm twenty still inside my mind.

Gwyneth Jones (Macclesfield)

Another Place
(Antony Gormley's Iron Statues)

What are they looking at - just out of reach
Antony Gormley's Iron Men on Crosby Beach?
From Waterloo to Crosby and on to Formby shore
They stand erect, a hundred men and more.

One man, in Liverpool football kit stood looking out to sea
Another had on a mortar-board - when Cherie B got her
honorary degree!
And yet another man was seaweed-crowned
Like a naked Caesar laurel-wreathed around.

They stare into the distance - Gormley's alter egos,
As they watch the ships and wonder at their cargoes.
Container ships are slowly sailing past
As long as blocks of houses - and as vast.

Ferries to Ireland and the Isle of Man move swiftly by
The Iron men just stare with sightless eye.
These statues all stretched out along the shore
Give one a sense of space, of peace and something more.

Making one stand awhile and pause, like them
To value God's creative gift to men.
We see the Wirral coastline - Hoylake and New Brighton
The distance hills of Wales - the Snowdon mountain.

The sand dunes where the sand is really gold
And 'Waterloo Sunset', so lovely to behold.
It's close to Liverpool - so come, make haste
And visit Crosby and 'Another Place'.

Angela M Schroder (Liverpool)

Joy Of Cumbria

In this paradise, where I now reside
My heart swells, with enormous pride
Euphoria strikes, at sights I can view
The sun will shine, from skies of blue.

To see the hills, covered in white
Roaming the fields, which is our right
Sailing the lakes, on a passenger boat
Seeing daffodils, of which Wordsworth wrote.

Enormous forests, in which to get lost
Spectacular surroundings, at no extra cost
Rivers and streams, lakes and meres
The sights and sounds, which one reveres.

Each season, as it starts to unfold
The richness we see, of solid gold
The birds of prey, watching them feed
Migrating each year, then returning to breed.

The history of Whitehaven Town
Loads of mine shafts, now closed down
Egremont, with its yearly crab fair
The strange event called gurning, takes place there.

See where submarines were constructed in Barrow
Agricultural shows, you'll find a large marrow
Hear of John Paul Jones, at the Rum Story
A buccaneer who was never covered in glory.

Visit Keswick, where lead pencils are made
The taste of Kendal mint cake, will never fade
Maritime festivals bring folk, from far and near
And these take place, every other year.

A communal spirit seems to thrive
People determined the area will survive
A spot of tourists continue to embrace
That's why Cumbria is a special place.

B W Ballard (Whitehaven)

The Battle For My Mind

The battle has begun
Between Jesus' friend
And Lucifer's son
Good will win,
I'll be free of sin.

Look at the state I've been in
Fifteen years with a voice in my head
All alone in the world
I might as well have been dead
Living with this 'evil' in my head.

The battle has come at last
I'll fight all those demons
I'll take them to task
I'll no longer wear the mask
That mask that says 'hate'.

It's time to lose my fear
The fear of being 'here'
The fear of my own mind
To find out who I am
The truth to find.

The battle is nearly at an end
I've defeated the voice of Satan
Now Jesus is my friend
This crazy war is over
My mind has been set free.

Peace has come to my mind at last
It's the only way to be
I fought and fought the battle
The battle for my mind
It's so good to have my life back.

From now till the end of time
I no longer see the darkness
I only see the sun
Life is now for living
The battle has been won.

A P Richardson (Manchester)

My Wonderful Dad

Around the world in 97 years
That's how far he travelled in his long and wonderful life!
At the tender age of fourteen
He met lily, his late and beautiful wife
They would walk the four miles and back
To work at the old 'E Mill'.

Creating wealth from the cotton that they had spun
The masters, they grew rich in turn
From your sweat and tears
But the old frames are still now
And we can't turn back the years.

At nineteen they got married
And their long, grand love affair would last
For seventy-five years and more!
In honour of their long lives together
They received three telegrams from Her Royal Majesty!

They raised a family of four daughters and one son
Mum will be waiting at Heaven's great door
When he reaches his long journey's end
My wonderful dad, the Marathon Man!
Your loving son, Kenneth.

Kenneth Pendlebury (Manchester)

Next February

Next February will be different.
It will not fool me, like the previous fifty.
This time I will be ready, however it mistreats me.

Autumn thrilled me once again with fancy hues
From shades of brown that made me wonder
If there were so many shades of green this summer.

The resultant skeletons make me shiver,
But I know it will be done by Christmas
And January will freeze and go exactly as expected.

Poor January, blamed for the ills of winter.
At its end, it will be safe to de-hibernate and venture.
The snow drifts gone, the ice caps melted,
Heavy coats brushed, bound, hung, rested,
Thick woollens, gloves and hats, washed and stashed.

Then February comes – with its secret R.
R for the *wreck* it leaves me, with the silent W
For that unexpected extra winter that comes each year,
Just as I think that winter's over
Because February is here.

T I Hill (Manchester)

A Poem For Mum

When we had troubles in our life
And we were sad and blue,
Our mum would *always* be around
To help us make it through.

When we were afraid and nothing seemed
To help us calm our fears,
Our dearest mum was always there
To wipe away our tears.

We sat and talked of bygone years
And how friendship stood the test,
You shared our joys, you shared our tears
You always did your best.

Memories are precious,
They give us strength
They help us carry on
I love you, Mum
With all my heart
And miss you now you've gone.

Joan Beer (Manchester)

Wonderings

Have you walked through a shaft of gold sunlight where rivulets kiss the soft sand
Or wandered alone in the twilight and yet felt the touch of a hand?
Have you dreamed magic dreams of enchantment when the hour came for day to depart
And then in the chill of the evening, felt a glowing warmth weave around your heart?

Have you gazed at the wonders of Nature, filled with awe at their marvellous fashion
Wondering whose hand had traced their formation and guided by which kind of passion?
Were the mountains in angry mood chiselled, or the wild waves created in mirth?
Was it love that absorbed the Great Maker when He fashioned the Heavens and Earth?

Have you known anything of the mystery that unfolds with love's tender embrace
Or discovered why men reach for stardust, when smiled on by some lovely face?
Do you know when a wounded heart's breaking, what happens to all the sad tears?
Do they find other eyes for safekeeping and live endlessly on through the years?

Can it be that the fair face of Helen, which launched countless ships long ago
Still lives with its tenderest beauty in the dear face of someone we know?
Maybe moments in Time and Experience give us each greater wisdom to see
That although we may wonder and question, there is so much remains mystery.

Vivienne Joyce (Liverpool)

Cumberland Song

Let's sing a song of Cumberland:
Of mountain, fell and scree,
With placid lakes - and windswept hills
And miles of sand and sea . . .
Oh, wind that blows the heather's scent
Blow Cumbria's song for me!

Let's take a look at Cumberland:
Come, join me and we'll gaze
At rocky crags and towering peaks
That pierce the morning haze . . .
Oh, mist that veils old Skiddaw's head
Let Cumbria's beauty blaze!

A county for all seasons, this,
With mountains - winter-white;
And in the spring - the poet's joy -
With daffodils alight!
Then scudding sails on summer lakes
Till autumn's russets bright.

Let's raise a toast to Cumberland -
To sturdy Herdwick sheep
That roam the fells from Birker Moor
To Honister so steep;
May eagles, foxes, wheeling gulls,
Her natural wildness keep!

From Carlisle's rosy castle
To the sands of Bardsea Beach,
From Scawfell to Blencathra
And as far as the eye can reach,
Her artists, poets, friendly folk
Will Cumbria's beauties teach!

Mary Dimond (Egremont)

The Simple Life

When I retired from work in 2003
I thought that now I have time on my hands
I can do all the things I have wanted to do
Such as visit far-off lands

Could I realise a dream I have had for years
To travel on the Orient Express
Or have a starring role in 'Coronation Street'
Pulling pints in The Rovers no less

My list of things I'd love to do is endless
Could I work for the BBC
I see myself as a Radio Presenter
With millions of people listening to me

There is one thing on my 'to do' list
That I am thrilled to have done
And that is publish my own Slim Volume of poetry
Which was such enormous fun

Writing poetry I find so therapeutic
And I really must confess
I go weak at the knees when I see my work
In the fabulous anthologies published by Forward Press

I feel sure that most of my 'to dos' will never happen
And will be nothing more than a fantasy
I have six granddaughters, my poetry and very loyal friends
Yes, this is the life for me.

Jackie Richardson (Kendal)

St Barnabas' Diamond Jubilee -
A Thanksgiving

Thank you for St Barnabas' Church and all that it has meant
For the vision of those gone before and their great commitment
Thank you for the last 60 years
For times of joy and times of tears
For the saints now at rest with You
Who through trials and tribulations saw the venture through

Thank you for the person who sold Bredbury Hall
Upon the understanding it was to be a church for all
Thank you for the 'Daisy Field'
That had a harvest for You, to yield!
Thank you for the builders who erected the building here today
A shelter and a refuge for Your church to praise and pray

Thank you for the people who have laboured here for You
Who have done their best to serve You, both priest and laymen too
Thank you for the people You have brought through our front door
We pray that as the years go by, there will be many more
Help us to continue the work, so long ago begun
Send Your Holy Spirit to live in everyone

Make us all encouragers and spreaders of Good News
Always ready to help - and listen to others' views
Lord, fill us with Your Spirit, so we will truly glow
And the people of Lower Bredbury will be sure to know
That St Barnabas' Church, now 60 years old!
Will be happy to welcome them into the fold.

Rita Robinson (Stockport)

The Dragonfly

Every summer a dragonfly visits
Bouncing, lifting and diving, he flits.
Camouflaged stripes echo the greenery he lives,
With a translucent shininess, which gives.
For he comes up close and his presence is real,
A revelatory, unconcealing that does reveal.
Flying here, now flying there, where he might
Embark on incisive incisions through the sunlight,
Every year he does appear,
A testament to time and its passing.
For like the summer and those before,
He too, will disappear.

Martin Jenkins (Ellesmere Port)

Aunt Maude Blues

Lavender and lilac days
Court musk and opium nights
I embrace tranquillity
While the sultry air delights
I dance at the foot of Mother's bed
In the antique mirror pirouette
A graceful curtsy and bow of head
With rapturous applause I am met

Nineteenth century wardrobe
Old mothballs mingle with must
Great Grandma's 'Little Women'
Covered by decades of dust
My mind wanders back to its childhood
Into a family tragedy
Grandfather Albert he was no good
Committed murder atrociously

My mood of gloom disrupted
By laughter from schoolchildren
I gaze down from the window
And wish I could be with them
As the hours pass and midnight strikes
An eerie stillness pervades her room
Switch off the light, draw back the curtains
One-way conversation with the moon

I must take stock of my life
Before I run out of time
Fear of the words 'if only'
Inhabit my troubled mind
If only I was like dear Aunt Maude
If only her spirit possessed me
I'd kiss my daydreaming days goodbye
And break the shackles of fantasy.

Pauline Ilsley (Prenton)

Skyline

As I sailed up the Mersey through swirling mist
I gazed at the liver, a sight not to be missed
With a lump in my throat, I knew I was home
I vowed then, that never more would I roam
Though I've travelled far and travelled wide
Never once forgetting my own Merseyside
I've seen places of beauty and some very pretty
But there is none to compare with my native city

The street musicians, or the one-man-band
Can now be heard playing in our club land
The St Johns Precinct, a shopper's delight
The food stalls bask in a blaze of light
Selling exotic foods from distant lands
It's like Paddy's Market, but with its covered stands
Where many happy hours could often be spent
With bargains to be had for just a few pence

Times have changed since I was here last
Old, familiar places are disappearing fast
Multi-storey flats stand like concrete hills
Taking the place of some old flour mills
The planners dream castles now in reality
The skyline has changed but not our dignity
Everyone now is living at a quicker pace
Liverpool to me, is still a wonderful place.

William Reilly (Liverpool)

A Dog's Best Friend

Hello! I'm Cash, a modest chap, tho' handsome in my way,
I've lived in these parts all my life and I don't have plans to stray.
The laid-back life just suits me fine, it's clear by my demeanour
And you'll see me walking every day with my faithful pet, Georgina.
There springs to mind one winter's day, quite frosty, I recall,
We went on the embankment for a game with Gina's ball.
The exercise is good, I find, it gives the legs a stretch
And seems to please Georgina, yes! She loves a game of fetch.
But that day things were different, the ball bounced out of sight
And when I bounded after it, the brambles caught me tight.
Down, down I went, twelve feet or more, straight into the canal,
I'm drowning, was my only thought, then I spied my little pal.
Along the grassy bank she sped and jumped into the water,
Thinking back now, I must say, 'It was just as well I'd brought her.'
Moments later all was well, soon Gina had me free,
I could tell she was delighted by the way she looked at me.
I didn't bother swimming, lest ungrateful it may seem,
But let her carry me ashore, as I planned this little scheme.
A thorough shake to dry my coat, a scratch or two and then
I'll find a stick to play with and we'll do it all again.
Gina didn't seem too keen, she said, 'Once is enough,
I'm squelching in my wellies and I'm running out of puff!'
All this was witnessed by a man, but offer help? Not he,
His only comment as we passed, was 'What's her pedigree?'
Is that the time? I'll have to go, I'm ready for a snooze,
But first I must walk Gina and rush back to catch the news.
Of adventures in future, I'll be sure to let you know,
But in the meantime, you take care, goodbye now, cheerio.

Beryl Thornbury (Stockport)

Travel'er

I'll travel, far an' wide
To be, by your side
Across many ocean's blue
Just for being with you
My family

Paul, Rachel, Thomas, Charlie
Smiling faces
I'd wish, I could see
Once more from
Across the sea

New Zealand
This place for me
Flying, darting across those skies
Wondering whatever
Night-time, daytime
It's sure to be

Check your watches
Captain's cries
Through his loud speakers
Amongst those clouds

Meeting, chattering
People you've met
Eating, sleeping
Oh! Dear me
Relaxing, exercise a must
Reading, thinking
Being in touch

You're on your way
Once more this day
Time to be strong
It won't take long
Before I see my family.

Gail Rowan (Widnes)

Brindleheath

The houses are now demolished
As they sprawled across the Irwell Valley,
Old, decaying images of yesteryear silhouetted
                darkly across the jumbled skyline,
Chimneys that once smoked, old factory roofs
                Hovering over half-demolished terraces
That have been Salfordians' homes for centuries,
A viaduct humps like some gigantic eel across the
                wasteland that was once streets
Canal full of litter and bricks
Derelict lamp posts at drunken angles
All Taste of Honey and Love on the Dole images
                rolled into one landscape.
Children once played in the rubble, building rafts
              in the sea of debris between factory walls.
The streets are empty and strangely silent
Paper is caught up by the wind and like tumbleweed
                in some forgotten Western
Drifts across the man-made desert
A weak sun glints through rafters casting faint
                shadows on timeworn setts.
A few pockets of life still survive.
A giant dog rests in a window, is aroused by footsteps
A woman carrying a bag moves across the street,
                stepping over bricks and glass -
'Spuds, 12p a pound! Disgusting!' she shouts, as she
            unlocks a battered door and enters a shabby hall.

Philip Loudon (Salford)

Tears Of Life

Give me your hand to hold, cry no more tears,
I alone will give you strength,
For your worries I, will carry your cross,
For everything I offer thee, my life, my home
My love for thee, hold my hand.
Together, we walk, a lifetime, of happiness
And eternal love, we walk the streets of Heaven.
Forever in God's heavenly love.
On Earth no peace of life, to give
Only hurt and forever sorrow,
Hoping for a new tomorrow.
Gone are forgotten cheers,
Not for me, not for you
All our promises are through.

Jennie Stott (Darlington)

Home Is Where The Heart Is

Climb the highest mountain
And reach for the sky
Or walk in the valley below
With that wonderful glow

Roam the lands and see the sights
From the Leaning Tower of Pisa
To the picture of the Mona Lisa
From Sydney Harbour Bridge
To an Arizona Ridge
From the Island of Samoa
To the Island of Alloa

Sail the seven seas
Feeling the fresh sea breeze
Or fly out into space
With the utmost of grace
Where the sky is blue
And the flight is true

But there is nothing like the feeling
You are concealing
The feeling of relief not of grief
The feeling when you've realised
What you have missed
The long years you have been adrift.

David Hamey (Manchester)

I See You!
(Dedicated to my wife - Niki)

When people look at you
They see what they want to see
When I look at you - I see
More than a mother, a wife and a friend
A beautiful young woman with feelings
With the most gorgeous smile
And soft and gentle kisses which melt my heart
When I look at you, what do I see?
I see the most beautiful woman
That God has ever created
I see you . . .

Andrew Rawlings (Oldham)

The Fall

I watched the fall
for a moment
life hung in a balance
then lost its grip and toppled
over the edge.
I imagined the fall
to be a slow, graceful process,
a floating, twisting
moment in time
but in reality, the fall was a
plummet,
fast and furious,
straight down,
hurtling as though in a hurry
to crash into the ground.
For this bronzed, autumnal leaf
life was over
but
I continued to watch
The Fall.

Denise Southern (Preston)

April 23rd

We celebrate today George slaying the Dragon
A good excuse, if needed, to stay off the wagon
'Tis the day Will Shakespeare was born; and also the day
                                                         he expired
So great were the plays wot he wrote; of his poems, we'll
                                               never get tired
Brian Boro, this date, was killed at Clontarf
Do the Irish still love him? They all say, 'Not half!'
To *this* Brian the day's special for reasons of love
'Twas when I tied the knot and on honeymoon made off
And the love for my wife's still constant and true
On St George's Day and the whole year through.

Brian Lees (Nelson)

Write It Down, So It's Not Forgotten

White it down, so it's not forgotten
cold winter is approaching, we have no food.
The enemy is coming.

The enemy is raping and torturing,
we can no longer survive this conflict.
Write it down, so it's not forgotten.

This place is being ravaged, destroyed, obliterated,
resistance is futile, we must leave.
The enemy is coming.

The old ones are resistant to the journey,
not wanting to leave their birthplace.
Write it down, so it's not forgotten.

Winter will make the journey impossible
across the mountains, we must not delay.
The enemy is coming.

This place was beautiful to live in,
now we cannot see a future for our young.
The enemy is coming,
write it down, so it's not forgotten.

Jean K Washbourne (Southport)

A Light Shines On Blackburn In Lancashire

Visit Blackburn, a great north-west town,
Resplendent in a multicultural gown.

Inter-faith dialogue is a shared goal,
Cathedral and mosques express the town's soul.

The Lantern Glass above the altar showers
Rainbow reflections during sunny hours.

The Council values civic pride,
Witton's beauty cannot be denied.

Offices, shops, King George's Hall,
Terraced housing and parks for all.

It's a grand place to work and live,
Blackburn has so much to give.

A kaleidoscope of great potential,
The town is close-knit and reverential.

It's vibrant, energetic, vast,
Come for the day, don't wait to be asked!

Visit the market, wander around,
Many a bargain is there to be found.

There's fish and fruit and beads and wool,
Bags, pens and pencils to use at school.

The shopping mall is being regenerated,
This investment has made the retailers elated.

Enjoy some Thwaites, relax and laugh,
It's the home of Rovers and Lancs. Telegraph.

Majestic, radiant, cathedral town,
Love embraces everyone as pure Light shines down.

Crystal Waters (Blackburn)

Blackpool Tower

A waterfall of light is pouring
down from the setting sun
onto a sea of hammered silver.

At intervals, upon smooth sands
crawl tiny insects shaped
like donkeys and humans.

In the East, a rainbow
embraces rain-dark houses, streets
and many rainbowed dinky toys.

The banal is transfigured
to mysterious marvels
by mere elevation.

Hope Bunton (Preston)

Lonesome

I think I can hear you calling,
or is it only in my mind.
The slight wind that moves the door,
makes me fancy you are there
'hiding' behind it.
But it's just those usual elements,
that happen all day long,
like wafted tissue papers
scurrying along the ground.
Love, you never were, Mr Glum,
on the contrary, you simply possessed,
good humour and fun,
full of devilment, 'no' more rumness,
happier still - when you teased a bit,
but 'twas only to 'make 'em laugh'.
Many times you were, the party's life and soul
you'll never know, how much you're missed.
Gone are those days of partying bliss.
But 'memories are forever', 'treasures to behold'.

Peggy Johnson (Liverpool)

Through The Haze

Slowly rising from a night of slumber,
Through the haze it penetrates,
Producing life-saving warmth and energy,
For the benefit of humankind.

Without its vital rays,
Our lives, would a sorry state.
It brightens the day and makes us feel good,
It makes us glow with happiness
And gives us the bounce of joy.

Its harmful rays can burn the skin,
When we have over-indulged.
Without its beneficial rays,
Flowers and produce would not mature.

It's a joy to see the leaves and grass,
Glisten and sparkle with the morning dew.
Like scattered fragmented diamonds,
Sparkling in the morning sun.

Burgess Jay Barrow (Preston)

Reina Of The Marshes

It was the *moss*. It claimed the winter rain;
And not just here or there, but everywhere
It spread for mile on mile. Only checked by banks
Which held the mighty river
Forging on in endless time. The moss;
It grew and spawned in microscopic strands
And cupped and coveted its prize.

It was the *light* which changed the flow. It shed an enigmatic glow
Awakened by a sun whose season's equinox had just begun
Parading light, arising from the moss
Stirring each and every bud; or leaf
Or lichen lying on the wood.
Creating all as new
The light began to grow and grow.

It was the *dew*. It rose to form a mist and change a life.
A mist enshrined in essences of pine and herbal scent.
The moss released its potent crushing force.
Not one, but more who fallen, falling still
Became its captive slave
To that pure hour in nature caught
Enraptured in that aromatic state.

The salty earth reclaimed the clinging moss
And waited . . . waited for another year.

Christine Dodding (Preston)

Ethereal Pause

It's midnight in Elswick
And all you can hear,
On the current of crystal,
Which is this time of year.

Is the crackle of past, present
And things yet to pass
And the munching of sheep,
On the frost-christened grass.

Of wind, there is none,
Not to even a sigh,
But the angelic orchestra,
Glittering on high;

Communes loud and clear
And in terms which compel,
With all souls and in the immortal,
Music of a spell.

Di Wade (Blackpool)

A Day Beside The Sea

Eee the day I went to the seaside
With my best friend, May
'Twas a sunny day
Walking along the sea front
Eating fish and chips
Staring out to sea at the passing ships
Looking up at the seagulls swooping and looping
Jabbering high in the summer sky
Taking off our shoes to run barefooted along the sand
To paddle in the sea
We could hear the melody of a brass band
Then bottling up a bit'a sand
To go away and remember the day
May and me spent the day beside the sea
Eee it were grand! Eee it were great!

Olwen Hornby (Heysham)

A Special Time

That special time has evolved once more,
To dig out, the ladders from the garage again
For in the loft, is where I must climb,
To bring down the boxes small and large

For without them the scene would be bare,
Taking their contents out is such a joy,
Different colours, long and some much shorter,
Glistening, like silver and gold, when twirled

Baubles too, with many colours to match,
A tree that has its own snow, so real,
Crackers placed along its branches, so many,
Along with chocolate treats to tempt

Streamers, long and curly, to show off
Ouch! That one should have gone in the ceiling
And not really in the finger, that pin,
Holding up a decoration to please us all

Lights on the tree, changing in different colours
An angel on the top, looking down,
Presents, many under and on the floor
Christmas is now on its way

Children showing so much excitement,
Many letters wrote and sent to Santa
With wishes of things that are wanted,
Some are granted, while others a disappointment

A special time for us all to say
And be together without fear
Holding a glass in our hands to celebrate
A very merry Christmas and happy New Year.

S J Davidson (Heysham)

Lancashire, My Lancashire

There were chimneys pointing to the sky,
Belching soot and grime
And flecks of lint clung to one and all
In good King Cotton's time.

There were foundries with their furnaces
Made the night skies red
And sparks outshone the brightest stars
To light our way to bed.

The artisans would sweat and toil
Hammering night and day,
The noise mixed with the clattering sounds
Of clogs on cobbled way.

Many a man went down the mine
To work from dark to dark
And every town had bands and choirs
To out-sing the soaring lark.

There were sludge-filled, poisoned rivers too
Killing fish and fly and seed,
This was a filthy Lancashire
Created by Man's greed.

But now all this is past and gone
No more clogs walk cobbled lane,
No more sparks, no stench, no noise
And yet we've many a gain.

For now we work with microchips
In air-conditioned rooms,
No muck, no mire, nor stoke-hole fire
And no one tends the looms.

With air to breathe 'neath sunny skies
Green hills with many a tree
And dancing rivers flowing clear,
'Tis a county that suits me.

Adrian Yates (Leigh)

George's Ghost

When Orwell took 'The Road to Wigan Pier'
He painted a picture so grim,
No doubt, at the time, what he penned was true,
The aspect seemed hopeless to him.

With mean, crumbling dwellings, poverty rife,
Folks desperate, desperate lives,
Miners depicted as loutish and coarse,
Children hungry and worn-out wives.

But let George's ghost walk in Wigan today,
He would see with wondering eyes,
A bustling, thriving, progressive town,
Far removed from coal dust and pies.

A town with a future, he could not know,
But one not forgetting its past,
The Orwell image is long outlived,
A new Wigan is here to last!

Eric Holt (Bolton)

Museum Of Hope

Cars race for the lights,
Inside a biscuit-stone building steeped in sunshine,
Sunlight gilds embroidered banners;
Gleams of golden thread depict
In coloured fabric fields and factories
What's made, mined or grown
By the marching people
Gazing from the bright banners,
But no longer in the street,
They are marching no longer.
They're caught, canned and racing down the road
All together, but all alone
In separate safety cages
Past the Museum of Hope.

What does it mean to anyone,
This temple of long-dead causes?
I may as well sign the pledge, buy 'War Cry', call you
'Sister', 'Brother', or worst of all, a 'Worker'.
Who yearns for the herd?
That's right. Nobody. And if you don't like it,
'Comrade',
Take the bus
To the Museum of Hope.

Me, I have my Heaven,
Up my drive
Tiled with setts stolen from Salford I glide
Under my molten lights
Under my watching cameras
Under my garage roof.
Keep off my land.
I've closed the ginnel, I've blocked the path
And fenced the pond;
The new enclosures.
I don't worship nature, I'm no pagan -
There are horses in my field, but no lilies.
God is money.
God
Is
Money.

Trust me. Trust me, that's all there is.
Everything else is left behind
In the Museum of Hope.

In a bubble of bright noise
I can watch, buy and drive.
Fearing the honest velvet darkness,
I banish the dark under molten lights.
Fearing silence,
Soft and fresh as a cold breeze,
I crush it under engine hum,
Under synthetic racket,
Running the clock down with DJ's babble.
A cellist at a chimps' tea party
Would be unheard, tails or no tails,
But luckily
So is the single bell of our loss
Tolling, tolling on the night breeze.
I'm entranced by the triumph of Numbers and Things
And in my trance
I'm buried alive in my beautiful car
Thinking I'm as free as the birds in the poison air.

What am I thinking?

Like a bird, it's gone.
Like a soft bell afar in the night.
But that's not a problem:
Even the thought that it isn't all right
Can go on the wall in a clip-frame
In the Museum of Hope.

Peter Rigg (Nelson)

Grandson Without A Dad

Tread softly, he's asleep,
serene and calm,
where you and I can keep
him from all harm.

We started off as two;
now we are three.
Our dream has now come true
so look and see.

Bewitch the baby boy
you brought to me.
Don't treat him as a toy
so painfully.

Hid dad went far away
but he was wrong
so now you're here to stay
where you belong.

His tiny body lies
in softest wool
and when I hear his cries
my heart is full.

Soft skin and rosy cheek,
silky to touch;
so tragically weak
he needs so much.

In trouble, toil and strife,
good times and bad,
this boy can share his life
without a dad.

Nancy Reeves (Blackpool)

Resolution

I go into my garden, full of zeal
That is, until I see the weeds - so kneel -
Wincing, I settle to my task,
No rain, or too much sun, is all I ask!
How proud, I later feel, as borders (weedless) flourish,
At least until my 'inner man' requires a nourish.
Alas! My knees, once bent, will not unbend
And I am forced to shout for help, from some kind friend,
To lift me up and help me get inside
The only damage being to my pride
I think - 'I might have stayed out there for hours
Fixed in position, contemplating flowers!'
I vow, next time, I *will* avoid humiliation
I *will* remember, old limbs do not function well
And tell myself the weeds must, go to Hell!

Joan Evans (Upholland)

Manchester Melancholy

Midnight slips her black velvet mantle around the city,
Her misty fingers trace
Along the viaduct
And curl around the tall, smokeless chimneys
Willing them to life.
Then chase the last tram along the line,
Muffling its retreat into the night.

Poking under the Irwell Bridge,
She urges the sullen ferryman across the canal,
To wake the restless souls at St John.
Her envious cheek grazes against the black windows
Of new warehouse homes,
Cracking their panes into a myriad of skeletal fronds
With her icy, scratching breath.

Dragging her torn petticoat of leaves,
She limps through foul, sulphurous pools.
Along Shambles Square, where,
She caresses the ancient beams
And churlishly tugs the fairy lights
Adorning its façade,
Tweaking the windmills outside the glass palace.

Once, ghosts of sickness and death,
Wailed cross Hangman's Ditch.
Victims of Peterloo and cholera . . .
Thick, choking soot, the rancid stench of disease and poverty,
Sullied the mean streets near Ancoats Lane . . .
Now long gone.

Atop the tallest building she sits
Cross-legged, hugging her knees against the freezing dawn,
Surveying her city below with dark-eyed fear.
Once riddled with grime and poverty
She dreads the new order
And mourns for the bleak past.

And then at last, she weeps . . .
Soft, gentle rain
Down onto the cold Manchester streets.
And all is as it was . . .
And ever should be.

Alison E Holland (Bury)

We Have Been Everywhere

We have done the whole of Europe
Been bored silly by the Nile
Explored volcanic islands
But we've yet to raise a smile
We have rediscovered America
Seen a canyon they call Grand
Been deafened by Niagara
The expressions still quite bland
Charmed by the snakes in Delhi
Watched the moon light the Taj Mahal
What was the reaction?
Completely abysmal!

Crossed over to Oceania
Stopped off at Singapore
In Oz we took in Ayres Rock
And found it all a bore
So then we held a conference
Next year we'd let the kids decide
Our family holiday destination
With their decision, we'd abide
They hardly thought a moment
In unison they screeched
Why don't we go to Blackpool?
Ride upon the Pleasure Beach!

Winifred Smith (Colne)

Closing Doors
(In memory of my cat, Cerces, 1989-2006)

Your brief illness caught me off-guard; an elderly
seventeen, it seemed you might go on forever.
The strangest thing was closing doors; the flat
arranged for your comfort; the hiding places;
cosy corners; soft blanket on the bed;
all doors open; like a welcome; saying;
I'm here, or here, or over here.
Now the place is full of space and silence;
once punctuated by your softness;
your light-footed walk; rhythmic purr.

I miss your morning vocals; that ruse of
getting me out of bed, so you could have
it to yourself; headbutts on my hand;
feline psychic advice; your queenly manner.

My eyes still look for you in familiar places;
I still walk around the space where your
food dish was.

Lynn Brookes (Preston)

A Lancashire Lass

I'm a Lancashire lass born and bred
In a little two up and two deawn,
Neaw feetur int front room weer black leadid grate
That glistened in't glow fru coal fire
In't fire oven tha did all thi bakin
Neaw I savour that smell ta this day
On tharth stud big pot wi dough risin
Tha baked all thi own bread i them days
On't cowd neets tha'd ar sit reawnd fireside
Discusin art farmily affairs
Thi mam ud be darnin or knittin thi fayther
Sit theer i tharmcheer,
Us kids sat on't flewer on't thomade peg rug
Wi toes curled up agenst fender
Wi long toastin fork weed tek turns doin bread
Tha wer nowt tasted better than toast dun on't fire
With a mug of hot coco fa supper

Neaw Monday wer alus a washday
Thonly clothes than wernt washed thi had on
Thi neer had no fancy contraptions
No little buttons fot press
Just dolly unt tub un thouwd rubbin board
Yer arms un back did aewt rest
Thi whites wer aewlus dun special
Thi wer boiled, dolly blued un then starched
Thn thid ring aewl thi clothes int wood mangle
Un peg um awtside int backyard

Friday neet wer a reet big occasion
It wer neet thi awl ad a bath
Thon suite wer tin bath ung aewtside on't back war
Thi weernt dirty i them days thi knows
Thi'd fill it ter top wi ot water
Then scent it wi carbolic soap
Aewt kids hair ud be washed un fine toothed combed
Ont Sunday,
Just in case Nitty Nora cum schoo on a Monday
Wi recycled eawl eawr own paper,
Cut up in neet little squares
Thi'd thred it awlt gether

Loop it wit string
Then ang it deawm yard ont lavatory dower
Uz kids made aew eawr own entertainment
It wer a case wot thi neer ad thi neer missed
Wid chalk on't wood top int brite colours
Spin it un it it wit whip
Play hop scotch, piggy, un reawnders.
Wit bag ur glass allies wi spent heawrs playin merps
But Satday wert thilite uv every kids wick
Off tert local bug heawrs thid go
Clutchin thi towfee in one hand and in tother thi threpney joe
Tarzen, Roy Rogers, un Trigger awe cowboys un Indian film
But best uv awr wer Flash Gordon, un the
Dreaded cloack figure uv Ming.
Gluwd tar thi seat wi excitement, reel ud start running eawt
Therd be won aewl mighty commotion, kids wud stamp
Un thid boo, un thid sheawt.
Thed go wom really exhausted, but appy contented wit day
Thonly thowt in thi yed as thi made thi way wom
Wud bi wot thed bi avin fer tae

Neaw neighbours wer neighbours i them days
Thi neer ad ter lock thi front doower
Thayd pop in wi a cup fer some sugar
Un stay fer an hower ur mooer
Neaw I know thay aewl liked a good gossip
Maybe thod glass ov milk stout
But int good times unt bad times
Wit sleeves rolled tert thelbers
Them neighbours ud awlus elp ewt
Ard workin un onest wert thouwd Lancashire folk
Wi ther deawn to erth owd fashion ways
It wer the pits, un the mills that made Britain Great
Wi ther wit un ther mirth they wer salt u
The erth

I'm reet proud, I'm a *Lancashire Lass*.

Ivy Jackson (Newton-le-Willows)

Whit Monday In Runcorn

All the Sunday School children
in their best clothes parade,
they come from all the churches,
some in white dress and veil are arrayed.

Relatives come from far and wide,
to see the Whit Monday procession,
in which younger members take part,
it is a family tradition.

The scholars walk through the town to the park,
where there is a big funfair,
the children are given some refreshment
and everyone gathers there.

There are try your luck stalls
and a big coconut shy
and you get one or two goldfish,
if you have a good try.

There are swings and dodgem cars
and a big carousel;
the lady with the crystal ball,
your future will foretell.

Cries of, 'Hello Joan,
I haven't seen you for a while,
are you keeping well,
that's the style.'

'Look who is coming,
it's our Fred and Sue,
are you coming back with us,
we have so much to tell you.'

So we go back for that special tea,
two or three sittings there will have to be;
salmon, custard tart and apple pie,
the children in the background heave a sigh.

As Gran says, 'Some more trifle,
or another piece of pie.'
'Hey Gran, there will be none for us.'
But Gran has plenty more put by.

Yes, it's a great day,
enjoyed by young and old
and the tradition goes back many years
I am told.

Violet Astbury (Ellesmere Port)

Memory Lane

I recently decided to go for a walk, well my sister decided it really,
It was just a stroll on a sunny day, just my big sister and me.
We started to walk down this little lane across the way from
                                                                  my home,
I didn't know then that from that walk, such special memories
                                                                     would come.

We walked a while then came across a pond where bulrushes grow,
I remembered that scene from my childhood, so many years ago.
I could hear my mum say to me, 'Don't stand too close or you'll fall,'
A little girl in her Sunday dress, with lovely puff sleeves and a bow.

From there the lane should have taken us to the Pit where our
                                                                  dad had worked,
But over the years it all had changed, the Pit was nowhere about.
I thought about Dad walking home from the Pit, after working all
                                                                day down the mine,
He wasn't a robust man, but to a little girl, my dad was tall and fine.

His hair was black, he was lean and trim and his body had little
                                                                    black scars,
He was a man who did a man's job and he played the mandolin.
I could see him walking down the lane, on his face, tell-tale
                                                                 streaks of black,
He was going home for his supper,
He had a lump of coal under his mac.

He would put the lump of coal on the fire and we'd warm to its
                                                                crackling sound,
'A good bit of coal is that,' he'd say, 'from the best coal seam around.'

Two people I loved, not just Mum and Dad, but man and woman,
Husband and wife,
Living their time as we are now, in a simpler, less affluent life.

It made me remember when I came home from school
On cold winter days,
Our wooden table would be brought up to the fire,
The fire crackled as it blazed.

My tea was sometimes a piece of bacon and lots of bacon dip
The egg, whenever there was one
Was for Dad when he came from the Pit
'Dip it up with plenty of bread,' Mum would say, as she placed
                                                                               it there.
I wonder what my mum had for tea and if there was any to spare?
I hadn't been down that lane for more years than I can say
I really don't know why that was, but I am glad I went that day.

Mavis Wright (Astley)

Pauline

Here she comes, she's so exquisite, like a dream,
The most beautiful girl I've ever seen -
What's her name? That's Pauline,
Everything she does is caressed with care
Can I approach her? Can I dare?
Can I show the immortal words to show I care?
Can I say to Pauline that I care?
Always a warm welcome on her face,
Her dark hair neatly kept in place,
She's an aphrodisiac to my heart
How could I ever want to see her part
And step away and leave me with the rest of today?
Her image stamped inside my head,
Beautiful thoughts to take to my bed
And sleep the sleep of a thousand years
Every moment inside it, seems always full of Pauline's dreams
The day's reality yet to break
Not storm in her heart that I cannot break
The magic will surely not be swept asunder,
I don't want to hear the sound of thunder -
Only the sound of her voice
For me, the one and only perfect choice
Protected by wind, surrounded by sky
She's in my heart till I die
Her face portrayed a thousand times in light
To come with me safe and secure in the night.

T McFarlane (Liverpool)

Home

So much land and so much water keep us apart
But my dear old Ireland, you are always in my heart
Beautiful hills covered with morning dew
Enhance my already great love for you
I miss the smell of the burning peat
And the enjoyable cosiness of the heat
The legends and myths can be awesome in tale
With your luscious green, your beauty never does fail
You are as warm and tender as any woman's hand
You are my home, my first love, my Ireland
With people friendly, caring and kind
A place in my soul you will always find
My feet itch to again tread your sacred soil
Over my next homecoming I often sit and drool
Until then, I will miss you day and night
Till once again I stand in awe at your sight
Welcome home will be played in my heart's band
When next I'm with you, my dear, old Ireland.

Graeme Doherty (Nelson)

Safe Within

Gas jet splutters, turn the mantle low
Black grate a-shining, coal fire aglow
Brasses a-gleaming, hearth spick and span
While in her clean apron, sits waiting, my mam
Dad's worked through the night, his shift at the pit
His breakfast is ready, so Mam patiently sits
Tin bath on the hearth rug, the kettles are steaming
The towel's on the fireguard, as Mam, with face beaming
Hears Dad's voice saying 'farewell' to his mate
Hears the latch lift on the backyard gate
Worries forgotten, for Dad is safe home
Get the bath ready, work up a foam
Help scrub the pit dirt that sticks to his skin
The house comes to life, when we're all safe within.

Nona Watt (Bury)

Blessed Silver Chimes

In the Year of Our Lord 1981
On a cold winter's night, the snow gently fell,
I lost in a street under sky of Prussian blue
Stars like angels' watching sacred life run its course.
This my soul haunted by wounded ghosts
In despair a voice screams and echoes within.
Then my weary eyes were dazzled
Who is this woman I behold
Before my ravished heart of love.
Oh, spirit of mystery with scent of joy,
A warm vision of feminine amazing grace.
She had a rainbow in her eyes
Like a sign from God for His broken child.
Her beautiful face of a whitest dove
Brought me blessed peace from realms above.
You spoke to me and sowed seeds of hope
And red poppies bloomed under darkest clouds.
Your words so bright, like lightning strikes
We were carried to Heaven in a chariot of gold.
Oh, in ecstasy I saw the black Madonna smile
Then with her fingers of holy fire, she touched my lips.
I bowed and unworthily kissed her dark, majestic feet.
Then I brought back to humbly walk on Earth
To sing a new song of blessed silver chimes.
Sweet Jesus let them ring in all human hearts and minds.
Blessed chimes of love and peace, hope and faith
And with the sweetest of tears welling up in my eyes
I walked back home, gazing at the pure white snow.

Thomas Hull (Blackpool)

Baby

Baby holding onto Mummy who is being forced to kneel
Baby being pulled from Mummy, who is begging for her life
Baby who cries as he looses sight of Mummy
Baby who is thrown to a soldier who walks to a van.

Baby who is put into a room with no light in sight
Baby screams for Mummy, food and a hug
Baby is examined as he sits on a big lady's knee
Baby is in a waiting room with countless other parentless souls
Baby is given no food, no place to call home
Baby is taken to a room where other babies groan
Baby wakes tired and alone.

Baby is picked up by Aunty who holds him tight
She spits at the soldier with all of her might
Baby is taken home with no parents to hold
Baby loses sight of justice as baby gets old
He hates the country that ruined his life
He vows reprisals for his own child and wife
He warns others about the increasing death toll
He says they too must die to achieve the supreme goal.

They talk until late about the atrocities they saw
They talk all day long about the war
His wife comes into the room and begs his return
She pleads and pleads for the meeting to adjourn
He dismisses her tears and tells her to bring his son
She goes for the boy who is playing with a gun.

Boy hits out at Mummy when she takes it away
He'll never understand the meaning of innocent play
She holds him regretfully by the hand
She leads him to the leader of this war-torn land
The boy sits at his father's right side
He has unsurpassable pride.

My daddy will kill them all
He has heard the divine call
Who are they to come to our land?
Destroy our family and spill blood on the sand?

My daddy saw it all
They killed his parents and promised that our people would fall
They are all scared of him today
They should have left him alone to play
He wasn't always this way
But since the day his innocence was damned
His only truth has been blood that will sanctify this land.

The day of disaster came
His trusty servants blew them all to shame
It was not long after
That we heard absolutely no more laughter
They came to my daddy as I clung to Mummy
'Daddy don't go. Please don't hurt my mummy!'

Now I'm a boy whose innocence is lost
I will make you pay triple the cost
I will one day be a man
And I too will have a grand plan
Why do we fight?
Which one of us is ultimately right?

Kelly Darbyshire (Blackburn)

The Poppy

The poppy in her crimson gown, flutters on the breeze,
Wild and beautiful, a thing of God, she dances where she please,
With wayside grasses interweaved, floating on the air,
The green and red a wondrous message, an unspoken prayer
On Flanders Fields she has appeared, her loveliness displayed,
Where men have fallen, lives been lost, in death's gloomy shade
And blood was spilt for freedom's sake and men have breathed
their last,
Guns and warfare have had their way, at such tremendous cost,
Hate has done her terrifying deed and men have given their all,
War has taken lives so young, on battlefield they did fall,
The poppy blows her delicate blooms where men once died in pain
And the echo of their dying cries, moves o'er the earth again,
Her crimson, a visual reminder of their human blood being shed,
Bobbing on the gentle breeze, in the poppy's lovely head,
No flower stirs the thought of man and brings a fragile tear,
As she in all her splendour in remembrance year by year,
For God has placed her amongst the grasses, where soldiers
bled and died,
Blending yesterday with eternity that now only love abide.

June Hardman (Skelmersdale)

Thoughts

Sleep, it has eluded me, as my mind goes round and round
Wishing I knew the answers for the problems that abound
The minutes slowly ticking past, as night turns into day
And still I cannot think of reassuring things to say.

As a mother, I remember when my boys were only small
When they had little troubles, I could usually solve them all
It's not so bad when they fall out with little friends they know
Because before you know it, they've soon got them back in tow.

But then as they get older and pride starts showing its face,
Times aren't quite so easy and sometimes it is a race
To make them kiss and make up, before harsh words are said
For then it is much harder and comes the time we mothers dread.

'It wasn't my fault,' you hear them say, 'It's up to them to speak'
And days, soon they begin to pass and soon it is a week
And then the weeks turn into months and very soon a year
And before you know it, they never tell old friends they care.

For as a child they cannot know how quickly time goes past
And how important friendships are, we must work to make them last.
For something that's so precious, so often causes pain,
But that is where your strength lies and each of you can gain.

So don't let pride take over, sit down and work things out,
Don't try and find out who's to blame, there'll always be a doubt,
For none of us are perfect, whatever we may think
But if we row together, we'll stay afloat, not sink.

So as our families grow up, if we cannot give them much,
We'll share with them experience, with a loving, gentle touch,
For as long as we have each other and keep to each other's pace,
The ups and downs are surmountable and together these we'll face.

So, please read these words so carefully, they are all that I can give
And remember how we act each day, will determine how we live
And in this time of trouble, let us share one with another,
That is the thought in every heart, especially a *mother*.

Florence C Watkinson (Southport)

Bygone Days

Where have they gone to?
Those old cobbled roads
The clanging of wheels
As the men fetch the coal
Covered in dust, their faces all black.

'Three bags today,' they shout
'And one bag of slack.'
Children out playing
No fear of the roads
Boys playing marbles
The girls play hopscotch
Mums on the doorsteps
Watching them play
Chatting to neighbours
So much to say

Where have they gone to?
Those old cobbled roads
The sound of rag and bone man
Shouting for clothes
The kids ask their mums
For something to swap
To give to the man
For balloons, whips and tops.

No tellies or computers
To keep them indoors
No thick pile carpets
To put on the floor
Toast made on the fire
Oh, it tastes so good
And our mums would sometimes
Throw in a spud.

Gone are the days of
The old cobbled roads
They're covered in tarmac
To carry fast loads
Shiny new cars, mobile phones

Gas central heating
No need for the coal
Progress is good in so many ways
But it's good to remember
Those old bygone days.

Rita Smith (Littleborough)

Accents

You may come up from Somerset or down from Lancashire,
From Wales, Rhondda Valley on from Tyne and Wear,
A Londoner can spot the Irish, Scottish sound,
Hereford and Hampshire, a variety is found;
In accents broad or genteel, no mistaking the place,
Wherever one comes from, you may be traced,
A cockney voice will give away their home without a doubt,
But isn't this the case, what life is all about?
A variety of speech, a hint of the living,
A decorative covering for every human being,
Accent add a sparkle, another sound to cheer,
That gave us Blake and Bronte, Tennyson and Shakespeare.

Mavis Catlow (Nelson)

Honk If You Love The Lord

I bought a car window sticker today
Which read 'Honk if you love the Lord'
I stuck it in my car rear window
And marvelled as I got my reward

I stopped at a red light at a junction
My mind began to stray elsewhere
I never noticed the lights turn to green
Till all the horns started to blare

I guess they had all read my sticker
And I think they all wanted me to know
The man behind me honked his car horn
And screamed, 'For the love of God, Go! Go! Go!'

Then he slowly drove much nearer
He must have thought I needed a shove
So I honked my car horn a few times
To show him I shared in His love

I saw one man wave to me in a funny sort of way
With one of his finger stuck up in the air
My grandson once told me that was a good luck sign
So I waved one back, 'well, that's only fair'

It was then that I noticed the lights were green
So I drove off, not without pain
Because I noticed I was the only car through
The lights had changed to red again

I felt kind of sad to have to leave them there
After all the love we had shared that day
So I gave them all the one fingered 'good luck sign'
As I smiled and swiftly drove away.

G Snowdon (Wallsend)

The Whispering Trade . . .

In bus queues and offices, schools, parks and shops,
Chance meetings on corners -
The buzz never stops.
The voices are lowered, the eyebrows are raised
And we all take our share of the Whispering Trade.

For gossip is always in major demand,
Secrets and eavesdrops - new or second hand!
There are earfuls of tension all bidding for thrills,
Reluctantly granted or gleefully spilled.
Yet value is something they never retain,
Unless they're repainted and sold on again
And so, as the stories are played and replayed,
We all have our share in the Whispering Trade.

But then there are those who just flatly refuse
To take this delight in the neighbourhood news,
Preferring to hide in a corner or hole
And remember the promise - 'I won't tell a soul!'
Because, when you've something important to tell,
It's safer to keep a select clientele . . .
For good reputations invariably fade.
Friendships are broken, heroes are made,
Sensation is crowned and the truth is mislaid
And nothing can silence the Whispering Trade.

Emily Blyth (Sunderland)

How Bizarre

Schooldays, they are boring,
What are they for?
A man's expected to be hard
And there's a kind of war
Between the pure and the lovely,
The good and the kind
And the school bully
Who wants to control your mind,
How bizarre.

Criminals are our heroes,
People think they're cool,
You smash the bus stop windows,
You're the hardest kid in school.
A man comes out of prison, says,
'You've had a sheltered life,'
A boy wants to be like him
And now he carries a knife,
How bizarre.

Force you to stay on at school,
It's the best thing to do,
If you don't get your A levels
There'll be no chance for you.
Force you to aim higher, to university,
If you're still unemployed by then,
A teacher you should be,
How bizarre.

A school leaver can't read,
He gets a job cleaning floors,
You carry on a year or two
And another job is yours.
An engineer graduates from university,
He's unemployed for ten years,
With a fairly good degree,
How bizarre.

Malcolm Lisle (Gateshead)

Northumberland Street

The high street shops call my name
I spend and spend
Not thinking of tomorrow
Because I could be dead

My joy of life fills my body
I run into the shops
And try on clothes and shoes
Holidays fill my mind

As the crowds go home
The sky floods with light
Seats are empty
And the shutters are coming down.

Kenneth Mood (Newcastle upon Tyne)

Litterbugs

Day and night
They don't care,
Dropping rubbish
Everywhere.

Bottles, fag ends
Papers, tins
Stuffed in hedgerows
Not in bins.

Can rings, matches
Bubblegum, peel
Fish and chip cartons
Half-eaten meal.

Litter on paths
Sweets, apple cores
Cigarette packets
Bus tickets, straws.

Crisp packets,
Tissues, paper bags
Cardboard boxes
Dirty rags.

Plastic containers
Condoms, glass
Disposable nappies
Discarded on grass.

Litter in river
It never ends
Will they ever change
And make amends?

Jean Cumbor (Middlesbrough)

Full Circle

Why did you never hear me
All those times I cried for help?
When I hacked off my hair,
You said, 'That looks nice, dear.'
And carried on watching TV.
When I wore loose trousers
And big, baggy jumpers
On hot summer days,
You said it was 'just a phase'.
When I hid from the camera
You shrugged your shoulders.
When I made myself vomit
You shouted, but wouldn't listen.

I pause for breath,
Stare unseeingly at the woman
Sat hunched up, before me.
Drool spilling from your wrinkled mouth
And down your thick, brown jumper.
Your shaking hands twitch restlessly
On the arms of the chair.
Pain-filled eyes pleading helplessly,
Begging forgiveness and help.
But just as you were not there
For me,
So can I not be there
For you.

Clare Thompson-Lewis (Newcastle upon Tyne)

The Run

The agony, the pain, blood rushing round
Blistered feet, the pavement pound
The ecstasy, I'm still alive
A pint and a curry, £4.95

The agony of training, in the past
The day of reckoning, here at last
The ecstasy of anticipation keen
Time to board the Metro, 7.15

The agony of nerves, here at the start
Thousands around me, all taking part
The ecstasy of comradeship while we wait
The race is starting, 10.08

The agony continues, as on we run
Run for charity, join the fun
The ecstasy as donations pour
Miles to finish, only 4

The agony, the pain, blood rushing round
Blistered feet, the pavement pound
The ecstasy, I'm still alive
The time at finish, 3.25.

R F Trollope (South Shields)

Bamburgh Castle

Set high on a basalt outcrop
Above the beach's creamy sand
To the east, looking across the North Sea
To the west, guarding the land
During siege, never conquered, always free
On the ramparts, canons now in silence stand.

Within the rooms and vaulted halls
Carved chests and furniture grace gleaming floors
Walls adorned with ancestral portraits and scenes
Fine porcelain on shelves behind glazed doors
Figurines and enamel boxes displayed in vitrines
In the keep, weaponry from long-forgotten wars.

On the tower the brass hands
Of the blue-faced clock, mark the flight
As the hours forever onward go
The moon above on a clear night
And the floodlighting far below
Caress the ancient walls with light.

H J Slaiter (Milfield)

A Midsummer Moment

Soft waves lap blissfully
Onto a golden shore,
While wisps of soft air
Caress my cheeks, faintly pink.

Enveloped in a calm warmth
Gulls glide gracefully,
As sea and sky merge
Into a shimmering blue haze.

Time stands still
When the moment of
Complete harmony is captured,
Only to slip away on the breath of my sigh.

P J Wilson (Darlington)

The Rosy Cross

Spawned by seekers of a New Age,
    this rich archetype came to be
        one of the lights of the Golden
            Dawn. But today the bloom - stolen,
disenchanted - withers away,
    confined in staid fraternities.

Yet the mystic rose can be mine:
    a complex mandala unfolds
        its secrets, petal by petal
        and woos me to alchemical
wedding, transmuting my heart - signed
    by an immortal cross - to gold.

Peter Bramwell (Durham)

The Dream

Those eyes
Tuned like a radio
Observation, questioning me and my guilt
Feelings, where did you lose your feelings?
Did we ever have a dream, you and me?
Didn't we have a dream?
This gravity, another obligation of human nature
Can't hold me down
Your whisper was divine
My message from God
I never felt at home before
Not there or here
Where did everybody go?
Did we ever have a dream, you and me?
Didn't we have a dream?

Richard Alan Long (Gateshead)

Bryony Reads The Newspaper To Grandad

Says here, Grandad, in The Gazette -
Russian convoy sailors to get medals
Weren't you on that, in a corvette?

Aye - I did my bit for Uncle Joe,
Good old Stalin - means Man of Steel
'Twas Russkies that beat Hitler, y'know.

Says here, Grandad, on page four -
During fifties Stalin's spies
Mapped Teesside in case of war.

Well - there's a right irony,
Stalin bombing our steelworks.
Irony, geddit Bryony?

Bob Goodall (Guisborough)

Exmoor - My Garden Of Eden

When I moved house two years ago
As I drove with heavy heart
To leave behind all that I know
And from friends and family I would part

The place I will miss most of all
Runs along the southwest shore
Where you can hear the red deer call
It's my Garden of Eden, my Exmoor

Villages like Exford, a favourite of mine
Where a trout river curves its way through it
And the miles of forestry pine
What a lovely place to live, say those who knew it

A drive through the Doone Valley, going slow
From Lynmouth to the Porlock Bay
It's a single track road with long bends that flow
The gift shops, pubs and clotted cream teas, served all day

The humpback bridges over rivers and streams
The hills are steep and windy too
All these things are in my dreams
And so is the love I have for you.

Patrick J Horrell (Consett)

Feelings

Was it only yesterday
Across the sands of time
When first we met and
Hearts became as one?
Our eyes, visions of the
Soul - captured the
Moment - never wanted
To let go.

Or was this another time
Another place? When first
I saw your smiling face
When love was born and
Feelings spread - taking us
To dizzy heights of passion
Beyond compare -
Where only you and I were
There.

M M Armstrong (Carlisle)

Crossroads

Here I am at crossroads
wondering what to do
will this be a Christmas
that I'll remember amongst the few

Yesteryears were always lovely
for love was at the helm
keeping me in God's plan for everyone
which would never end

Now I'm left without answers
poetic or otherwise
for everyone knows their answers
and leaves wisdom to decide!

Beth Spinks (Guisborough)

An Ode To Jarrovians Everywhere
(Dedicated to St Paul's Church, Jarrow and the surrounding ruins of St Bede's Old Monastery. The anniversary of the Canonisation of the Venerable Bede which is held annually on 27th May)

Our education to write and read
Praise be to our Saint and the Venerable Bede,

In the midst of pillage and burning
The Monastery and the Monks carried on learning,

Ancient Gyrwy steeped in everlasting history
With legends of heroism, miracles and mystery,

A breed of folk that never cry
Inspired by a history that will never die,

Unharmed and safe, free from plunder and pillage
The Venerable Bede walked onto Monkton Village,

On this spot, sacred St Bede laboured at the well
Chores completed, tired and weary, he returned to his cell,

Centuries on, a world-famous shipyard mobilised
'Palmers of Jarra', worked by men, proud and organised.

Duncan Robson (Gateshead)

Remember Terri Schiavo

How do they know?
Who is to say?
Terri Schiavo may not have wanted to go along the yew-lined
                                            holy way,
she may have been quite happy,
            lying in her hospital bed, being fed, through a tube,
but now, she is conveniently dead,
            who, will ever know,
ask not for whom the bell is tolling,
ask instead,
the person who pulled the switch, why the body bags are
                                      being unzipped,
just hope and pray, a similar sickness bed, never confines,
                                        or beckons,
some harrowing spring day,
where bureaucracy tries to confound God's Holy Will,
            with nothing more to lose or say.

Robert Henry Lonsdale (Billingham)

Final Lullaby

Feel the warm, dry earth, cover your tiny feet,
Slip between autumn leaves and sleep.
No longer will I hear your cries,
Hear my final lullaby.
Dressed in a smock your granny bought,
Bootees of china-blue, a dried posy of forget-me-nots,
I could not know that you would die,
Hear my final lullaby.

Scott Maclean (East Boldon)

Just Passing Through

To the skirl of the pipes
through the misty glens
miles away from the wartime scene
we breathed in the smell of the lofty pine
aromatic - so sharp and clean.

We took in surroundings - out of this world
such balm the troubled mind
'til the RSM brought us back to earth
with words we considered unkind.

He accused us of not knowing left from right
an unpleasant character who
kept telling us we were not very much use
uniformed women - *taboo.*

He ranted and raved and lectured us
till we felt our ears would pop
as we marched along well past our mealtime
all feeling just ready to drop.

Yet, amazingly, in a very short time
we knew every twist, every turn
our footwork, he told us, in strangled tones
did us credit - so quick to learn.

Our training now finished - then 'passing out'
and 'postings' and train times declared
then off we were sent our separate ways
and many the friendships we shared.

With a smile, we look back on memories
of injections and blisters and such
the earwigs in bed kept us company
and orders that seemed double-dutch.

We wouldn't have missed it for anything
our life in His Majesty's force
we did what we could, were proud of the chance
to have trained at Camp Glencorse.

Kate Bylett (Middlesbrough)

Today's Bairns

They say today's bairns dorsint play in the streets,
An' sum of thim nivver gan oot,
Thi just stop in the hoose and watch the TV,
Cos tha's ower much vylince aboot.

When aa wuz a bairn, wi played outside aal day,
Aal neet if thi gi' wi' the chance,
Wi played roond thi lamp, slid doon thi pit heap,
An' came hyem wi nee seat in wa pance.

Wi played hide n' seek and tiggy on high,
Whilst the lassies played muggies and bays,
O's thi stud on tha heeds, wi' tha feet up the waal,
Dressed up in tha mothers aad claes.

The coal hoose and neeties wuz champion fo' hiddeny,
Os yi cud clime ower sumbodies waal,
Or put on ya wellies and plodge in the clarts,
Or play roonders wiv an owld bat an' baal.

But nite times wuz the best times when we hung roond thi lamp,
Wi did nowt much 'sept stand there an' taak,
Wi towld Pat an' Mick stories which med wi aal laff,
Oh, mevvies wid gan fo' a waak.

On iverry street corner an aad wife sowld sweets
N' lickorish and glasses o' fizzy,
Wi lukked in thi' windiz wi' wa noses pressed flat,
Tha wuz that much ti buy, ye felt dizzy.

Wi' thi' world like it is nu, sum kids nivver play,
Nivver skip, nivver jump, nivver run,
Thi just sit on tha backsides and watch the TV,
An' aa divvint caal that hevvin' fun.

Sum sit at computers playing' video games,
On tha own nivva taakin', just quiet,
An' as lang as thi divvint cawse neebody nee harm,
Thi just ask an' tha muthers'll buy it.

Nu aa ask ye is that any way fo' ti live?
On tha own an' stuck in the hoose,
When thi shud be outside wi' tha mates runnin' free,
An jumping aboot on the loose.

So fo' all them young bairns afraid ti gan oot,
I'm sure things must luk aafully black,
So ti all ee oot there afore it's too late,
Let's give thim tha childhood back.

John Stenhouse (Blyth)

The Jigsaw Of Life

Life's so much like a jigsaw, all mixed up, confused,
With its myriads of pieces, all so shapeless and abused.
With so many different colours and its sometimes flashing lights,
With its interesting dramas and its fascinating nights.
With its fluctuating moods and cacophony of sounds,
Its constant variations and its common daily round.
Life's like one great puzzle, with the answers hard to find,
A little bit of glory here and then a bit of grind.
A piece shaped like a tear and another like a frown
And yet another unfamiliar piece that seems to fit in upside down.
A sudden flash of humour, a sudden feeling of delight,
As just for one brief moment, life's pattern seems to come to light,
Then just as swiftly vanishes, as one important part,
Will not fit into the sky, but fits into the heart.
Life's puzzle's so confusing, but perhaps it's for the best,
That we cannot see the path ahead, its pleasures and distress.
If all were know that could be known, then how would faith survive?
How would simple trust in God and His love stay alive?
It's because life's such a puzzle and so hard to understand,
That we reach out through the darkness to grasp His loving hand.
For God has all the answers, He knows exactly where each part,
Fits into the picture, right from the very start.
The alpha and omega, the beginning and the end,
The King of kings and Lord of lords who deigns to be our friend.
The unknown path is known to Him, there's nought He cannot see,
From Him life holds no secrets, presents no mystery.
One day the pattern will appear, life's puzzle all complete,
The final, pieces all in place and sitting at His feet,
We'll worship Him who through life's maze, has led us night and day,
Up hill, through dale and valley deep, our rod, our staff and stay.
And so, Dear Lord, when life it seems presents no perfect plan,
But is a jumbled mass of pieces, beyond the skill of any man,
To form into a picture, or a pattern to complete,
Help us Lord to realise whilst sitting at Your feet,
That You have all the answers, You just know where every part,
Fits into the whole, from horizons to the heart.

W H Spry (Newbiggin-by-Sea)

Dualism

From Laugharne to Dublin, around the world and back,
writing between the lines of the politics of nature,
forming the words for the nature of politics,
for the likes of those who lived, unable to believe.
Not realising the hedonistic values of art
and denied the artistic desires of hedonism,
for the likes of those whose self-assurance is based in guilt.
Lambasted for writing and drinking to escape,
immortalised for escaping to write and drink,
from Laugharne to Dublin, around the world and back.

Dylan Thomas and Brendan Behan could you please explain to me,
if a bee lands in a bunch of nettles,
does the bee sting the nettles,
or do the nettles sting the bee?

Robin Bailey (Wigan)

A Life Of No Account

It would be so sad to die
And leave no scar on people's hearts
No ripple in the water of their lives
No footprints when the tide departs

To fade from view as a shadow
Leaves your side when the clouds
Shut out the sun

To leave no comma on their page of life
A mass of words but no mention of your lines

To be a muffled drum that never
Made a noise
A steady rhythm in quiet confines

To be a cold morning unwelcome
And kept outside
No one broken-hearted, bereft
And lost that you had died

No one to defend with indignation
To rage and question why
To stand around your lonely
Grave and cry

To disappear on the wind
Like an icy breath
A person of no mean, a life of no account
A wasted death.

Pauline Fazackerley (Barrow-in-Furness)

Ladybirds

It is midsummer. The man walking beside me is my father.
We are going to visit my mother in hospital. He keeps
stopping to point out narrow boars, bobbing about
on the canal, as figures in hats open locks.

I haven't heard most of what he has said,
I am searching for ladybirds in grass verges.
I am collecting different species as part of
a nationwide project. I slip them into a glass box
that magnifies their colouring and spots.

When I reach her ward, I count all my ladybirds
the ones from the hot bricks outside our house
and those from the towels at the public baths
and the others from the canal banking.
I keep counting in my head.

So I can't hear what is being said
about the daffodil petals that have fallen
like pills or the white hospital stockings.
I continue to count all night to prevent
thinking about how ill she really is.

Nicola Daly (Waverton)

The Tea Dance

We went to a tea dance
The ladies of sixty and over, we'd heard it was good
But the ladies outnumbered the gentlemen dancers
So we set to and did what we could.

We danced round the floor
Mrs Throstle, my partner, and me, chest to chest, so to speak
Till the music was finished and then we sat down
For a minute to rest our poor feet.

Then the band played a tango
And joy of great joys, a gentleman asked me to dance
I got to my feet, he was really quite charming
I knew that he fancied his chance.

Then the awful thing happened
It really was dreadful; I blush when I think of it now
We finished the tango, returned to our seats
And the gentleman gave me a bow.

But sadly (for him) this unfortunate man
(oh, know I won't look if we meet)
He leaned over so low in this gallant display
That his hairpiece fell off at my feet.

Joan Wheeler (Penketh)

I Remember

I remember wash days and the colliery rows
Lines hung with sheets and counterpanes
Billowing in the breeze like a flotilla of ships
Happily sailing away down the back lanes.

I remember the coal house and backyard
The posse tub and mangle both handled with care
A painted cracket beneath the tin bath on the wall
And the outside netty with its newspaper squares.

I remember the black range and its progy mat
The smell of washing and fresh baked bread
Teacakes and stotties rising on the hearth
A sizzling kettle and bairns shouting to be fed.

I remember the wheel house, ponies and trucks
The ever-growing slag heap and carbine lamps
Watching an army of weary black-faced miners
As they trudged homeward, cold, wet and damp.

I remember the weekends when the work was done
And children played dabbers or skippy in the sun
Parents and grandparents sitting at back gates
Chatting to neighbours, friends or workmates.

Greta Forsyth (Blyth)

A Teardrop From Heaven

I know I have to leave you but before I really go
Here are some memories of long ago,
Building sandcastles in the sand, swimming in the sea,
All I ask is, remember me.

Joy and laughter along the way, feeling so free
But when the time comes, remember me.
My dreams will be the moonlight that flits across the sky,
My smile will be the sun's rays that shines through the trees,
I'll whisper in your ear when the wind blows,
But when raindrops fall these will be my teardrops from Heaven
To say I'm by your side.
Remember the laughter, tears and joy along the way,
But most of all, remember me.
My life on Earth will be over but my love will linger on
And in return all I ask is, remember me.

Elizabeth A Wilkinson (Runcorn)

Beast

See your beast,
He plunges through the forest
Dark and deep,
His animus tongue throats a song
Of raw meat.
Time leads him to instinctive suicide
Of a species,
The rotting flesh smoulders
Like a funeral pyre,
A million vampire licks and my blood dries
Upon his terror kisses.
You called him to rise,
Wishing me no relief,
No love, no sleep.
You said the magic, blacked out the light,
Waited inside the circle
Until he was revealed
In darkest shades of fiery flicker.
Do you love your master now,
Now there is no retreat?
No love for you,
Your hatred so deep,
Deeper than the earth
Under his feet.

Glenda Stryker (Bolton)

Forward Press Information

We hope you have enjoyed reading this book - and that you will continue to enjoy it in the coming years.

If you like reading and writing poetry drop us a line, or give us a call, and we'll send you a free information pack.

Alternatively if you would like to order further copies of this book or any of our other titles, then please give us a call or log onto our website at
www.forwardpress.co.uk

Forward Press Ltd. Information
Remus House
Coltsfoot Drive
Peterborough
PE2 9JX

(01733) 898101